MOURNING FRIENDS AND FAMILY

Find gold keys in prayers and pick up
courage to continue with life.

FLORENCE ONOCHIE

authorHOUSE®

AuthorHouse™
1663 Liberty Drive
Bloomington, IN 47403
www.authorhouse.com
Phone: 1-800-839-8640

Published by AuthorHouse   11/03/2014

ISBN: 978-1-4918-7295-6 (sc)
ISBN: 978-1-4918-7296-3 (e)

Library of Congress Control Number: 2014917557

To speak at your event, summit, conference or convention,
e-mail me at fonochie@fnoproservices.com
Telephone Number 317-750-3434

www.florenceonochie.com
www.florenceauthorspeakercoach.com

This book is printed on acid-free paper.

Scripture quotations marked KJV are from the Holy Bible, King James Version (Authorized Version). First published in 1611. Quoted from the KJV Classic Reference Bible, Copyright © 1983 by The Zondervan Corporation.

DEDICATED TO THE MEMORY
OF MY DEPARTED LOVED ONES

Prayers, Photographs and Designs
by Florence Onochie

CONTENTS

INTRODUCTION

In writing this book, I have been inspired to use some of my favorite prayers, verses, proverbs, psalms from the bible and songs for they have been my greatest help in life, in times of joy and in times of sorrow.

It came to me as I was gathering information for this book to make the entire above channel of praying part of it in order to motivate, inspire and uplift you in whatever situation you find yourself, more especially as you mourn for your loved ones.

Always remember that prayer is the greatest weapon to fight any situation, there is nothing as powerful and it will lead you through and help you pick up courage again to continue on with life.

Best of Love
Remain Blessed
Florence Onochie

FAITH

"YOUR FAITH SHOULD NOT STAND IN THE WISDOM OF MEN, BUT IN THE POWER OF GOD"

1 CORINTHIANS 2:5

FAITH

As you bear this cross of grief and mourning for your departed loved one, remember that your faith will play a very important role in your life now.

WHAT IS FAITH?

Faith is the substance of things hoped for, the evidence of things not seen. It is your working energy. Faith will take you the stairs that love has built and looks out the window which hope has opened. When you have faith, it will strip the mask from the world and reveal God in everything for you. Give the Lord your entire heart and trust the creator for all you have not seen. Remember, that faith is not knowing what the future holds but knowing who holds the future. It is to believe what you do not see and the reward of this faith is to see what you believe.

Now, in sharing in your loss through my faith and prayers, we walk with the Lord on the way of the cross.

In our prayers, let us ask God to be our real and best friend as we go through this time of loss.

Let us ask Him:
To be with us
To send His spirit to us
To give us His healing touch
To hurry and help us
To renew us
To inspire us
To handle us with care.

HOPE

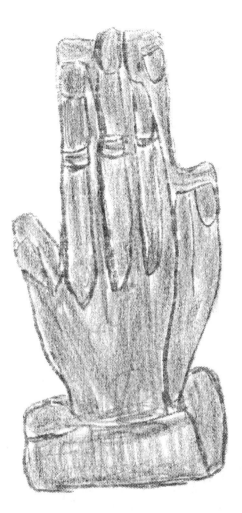

"BLESSED ARE THOSE WHO MOURN, FOR THEY WILL BE COMFORTED"

MATTHEW 5: 4

HOPE

Rekindle your hope in the love you shared with your departed loved ones. Hold on to what is left, be it your children or other memorable things you shared together. Expect your prayers to be answered in wondrous ways. Pray that the dry seasons in life will not last and that spring rains will come again. Remember that where there is life, there is hope for comfort and that hope is everything that is done in the world.

May the Lord comfort us and be close to us. May He show us His tender mercy and renew our hope and trust in Him.

The Lord cares for our loss, our grief, our tears, and all our sufferings. He will find a way to comfort us with His everlasting love.

Remember, that the Lord will always hold us in his arms, and shower us with his everlasting love. He will listen, care and embrace us with all our needs at this moment in time.

LOVE

"GOD IS LOVE"

1 JOHN 4:16

LOVE

In mourning, we all search for the hug of God, our ultimate true love. He is our Father and also our Mother. God is our lover, our longing, our flowing stream, our sun and we are His reflection.

"My soul finds rest in God alone, my salvation comes from Him. He alone is my rock and my salvation. He is my fortress, I will never be shaken".

Psalm 62: 1-2

Remember, that it is only in God that we find that special love, comfort, shelter and peace of mind. He is the strong tower, and the righteous run to the tower is safe. He is the God and there is none like Him.

"God is our refuge and strength, a very present help in trouble. Therefore, we will not fear, though the mountains be carried into the midst of the sea, though the waters there of roar and be troubled, though the mountains shake with the swelling thereof.

Psalm 46: 1-3

God is that special someone that you need to hear your prayers now. He is that special someone that is everywhere and that special someone that will care for you and answer your prayer from anywhere and at any time. He is the ultimate supernatural hero, the ultimate outsider, and the ultimate immortal.

"I am with you always, even to the end of the age"

Matthew 28:20

Prayers

"ASK AND IT WILL BE GIVEN TO YOU. SEEK AND YOU WILL FIND
KNOCK AND IT WILL BE OPENED TO YOU

FOR EVERY ONE WHO ASKS RECEIVES, AND HE WHO SEEKS FINDS,
AND TO HIM WHO KNOCKS IT WILL BE OPENED".

MATTHEW 7: 7-8

PRAYERS

Now, let us look at the different ways we exercise and pray for our depart- ed loved ones and ourselves left behind.

WHAT IS PRAYER?

Prayer is longing of the soul and the exposure of us to God. A soul without prayer is a soul without a home. Prayer unmasks, converts, compels and sustains us on the way. Prayer does not change God, but it changes him who prays. We can pray anywhere, for God can answer our prayers from anywhere and at any time. Remember, that prayer is an art to be cultivated, not an instinct to be followed. Secret prayer is the best of all prayers and the greatest of all is patience.

It is very important that we remember to call God with His different names when we are praying. CALL ON HIS NAMES, PRAISE HIM WITH HIS NAMES, AND CALL HIM THE:

BRIGHT AND MORNING STAR
CHRIST
EVERLASTING FATHER
GOOD SHEPARD
HOLY ONE OF GOD
I AM
IMMANUEL
JESUS
KING OF KINGS
LAMB OF GOD
LION OF JUDAH
LORD GOD ALMIGHTY

LORD OF LORDS
MIGHTY GOD
NAZARENE
PRINCE OF LIFE
PRINCE OF PEACE
RABBI

SON OF DAVID
SON OF MAN
TRUE VINE
WONDERFUL COUNSELOR
WORD

Let your first greeting of the day for example,
Good morning
Hi
Hello
Kedu
Ekaro
Etc

Be to your heavenly father in form of prayers. Before you go to bed, give your troubles to God. He will be up all night anyway.

In praying, ask God for what He thinks is good for you not what you think is good. Do your best in your prayers and live the rest for God to worry about and take charge in your life.

In all you do apply the favorite right view, right aim, right speech, right action, right living, right effort, right mindfulness and right contemplations. Realize that in doing so, and with God behind us and His arms beneath us, we can face whatever lies before us.

"And we know that in all things, God works for the good of those who love Him who have been called according to his purpose"

Romans 8:28

Also, in your prayers ask the Lord:
To be your vision
To be your heart,
To be your savior
To be your best thought day and night
To be your light when you wake up and when you go to sleep.

"The Lord is close to the Broken hearted and saves those who are crushed in spirits"

Psalm 34:18

REMEMBER: DO NOT LET YOUR SORROW COME HIGHER THAN YOUR KNEES.

And the Lord reminds us:

"And whatever things you ask in prayer, believing, you will receive. The Lord is NEAR to all who call upon Him in truth,

He will fulfill the desire of those who fear him, He also will hear their cry and save them."

Psalm 145: 18, 19

FAITH
HOPE
LOVE

Remembering Our Departed Loved Ones In A Glorious Form

We all know that life and death are one, even as the river and sea are one. We also know that there is no event in this world of troubled life that brings us nearer to our God than the taking away from us of those we love.

Let us remember and pray for them in different ways. Remember our loved ones with a melody of flowers to ease the pain.

Let us pray that the Lord will forgive them and grant them eternal rest. Let us remember them transformed into divine image of God with glory.

And the Lord reminds us:

"Whoever offers praise glorifies me;
And to him who orders his conduct aright
I will show the salvation of God"

Psalm 50: 23

Lord You Gave Your Entire Self For Us.

Your wounds for our healing
Your sufferings for our faults
Your agony for our peace
Your forgiveness for our sins
Your thirst for our comfort
Your blood for our redemption
Your death for our life

For those that repent, you promised a place in heaven.

I pray that you grant my departed loved ones the gift of life with you and welcome them into your heavenly home. May they dwell forever with you in light, happiness and peace where every tear will be wiped away, where sorrow gives way to joy and there is no more suffering.

I make this request to you God with all my faith, all my hope and all the love I can bring to you at this moment.

PRAYER FOR BLESSINGS FOR MY DEPARTED LOVED ONES

Lord, I ask for my departed loved ones

Your blessings and favor

Your love

Your gift of eternal life

Your splendor of Glory

Your light, happiness and peace

Your forgiveness

Your grant of eternal rest.

And the Lord reminds us:

"Because he has set his love upon me,
Therefore I will deliver him:
I will set him on high, because he has known My name.
He shall call upon Me and I will answer him:
I will be with him in trouble;
I will deliver him and honor him"

Psalm 91: 14, 15

On this ground where our loved ones were given the final farewell, where the remains were returned to the earth, earth to earth, dust to dust. We pray that you grant them:

Your love

The joy of your peace

And eternal rest

And the Lord reminds us:

"But I do not want you to be ignorant,

brethren concerning those who have fallen asleep, lest you sorrow as others who have no HOPE.

For if we believe that Jesus died and rose again, even so God will bring with Him those who sleep in Jesus."

1 Thessalonians 4:13; 14

YOUR PROMISE THAT EVERY TEAR WILL BE WIPED AWAY

Lord, we ask that you wipe away all tears with your love. Comfort us in this time of sorrow. We trust in you and we hope that you will grant us who mourn blessings, love and peace.

REMEMBER:

"That Christ may dwell in your hearts through faith; that you, being rooted and grounded in love, may be able to comprehend with all the saints what is the width and length and depth and height; to know the love Christ which passes knowledge; that you may be filled with the fullness of God."

Ephesians 3: 17-19

FOR OUR LOVED ONES

We ask Lord for you to be good, kind, merciful, generous, gracious and gentle to them till we meet again.

REMEMBER:

"As the Father loved Me, I also have loved you; ABIDE in my love. If you keep my commandments you will abide in My love, just as I have kept My Father's commandments and abide in his love.

These things I have spoken to you, that My joy may remain in you, and that your joy may be full.
This is My commandment, that you love one another as I have loved you. Greater love has no one than this, than to lay down one's life for his friends.

These things I command you, that you love one another"

John 15:9-13, 17

GRANT OUR LOVED ONES ETERNAL REST

Lord, we ask that you grant our loved ones eternal rest and peace.
Let your light shine on them.
Let their pain and illness go forever.
Let their minds and hearts be renewed.
Let their trespasses be forgiven.
We miss their smiles. May their souls rest in peace. Amen

And the Lord reminds us:

"Be anxious for nothing, but in everything by prayer and supplication, with thanksgiving, let your requests be made known to God; and peace of God, which surpasses all understanding, will guard your hearts and minds through Christ Jesus"

Philippians 4: 6, 7

Finding That Shining Light

In this time of sorrow, Lord open our hearts, that your light may shine on us, so that we will understand the power of your love, and let your light overcome any darkness around us.

We know that you love us and we hope to see the light of the world through you in us. Amen.

And the Lord reminds us:

You are the salt of the earth, but if the salt loses its flavor, how shall it be seasoned? It is then good for nothing but to be thrown out and trampled underfoot by men.

YOU ARE THE LIGHT OF THE WORLD.

A city that is set on a hill cannot be hidden.

Nor do they light a lamp and put it under a basket, but on a lamp stand and it gives light to all who are in the house.

Let your light so shine before men, that they may see your good works and glorify your father in heaven".

Matthew 5:13-16

GLOBAL LOVE FOR ALL

Lord, we know that you will always love us.
Your love for us is eternal.
Your love seeks to save
Your love is for all.
Your love is for the living and the dead.
Your love is the hope of the entire world and we thank you for your love.

REMEMBER:

He, who does not love, does not know God.
For God is love. If God loved us, we also ought to love one another.
"For God so loved the world that He gave His only begotten son, that whoever believes in Him should not perish but have everlasting life."

John 3:16

LIFE'S STRUGGLE

As we pass through life struggles, grief's and sorrow, Lord, we ask that you renew the life in us, give us the new life after all these pain from the loss of our departed loved ones.

Also, for our loved one's departed, embrace them with joy and take away all strains and sufferings.

Thank you my Lord for all your love.

And the Lord reminds us:

"When you pass through the waters, I will be with you;
And through the rivers, they shall not over flow you.
When you walk through the fire, you shall not be burned,
Nor shall the flame scorch you."

Isaiah 43:2

Mourning?
Sorrowing?
Weeping?

Whatever it is, you know all about it. We submit all to you.

Lord, the heart that believes is the heart that grieves knowing it is always in your love now and forever.

We believe that your mercy, your love, your care will lead us through and deliver us all from any state of mind we find ourselves in this time of sorrow.

Finally, Lord you are the omnipotent, omnipresence and the almighty.
Hear our cry from our voices, we will rejoice in you.
Hear our cry and forgive us our sins.
Hear our cry and strengthen our faith.
Hear our cry and build our hope.
Hear our cry for we trust in you.
Hear our cry and grant us your love forever and ever. Amen

CHECK THESE VERSES OUT. I LOVE THEM AND I KNOW YOU WILL LOVE THEM TOO.

Blessed are the poor in spirit,
For theirs is the kingdom of heaven.
Blessed are those who mourn,
For they will be comforted.
Blessed are those who hunger and thirst for righteousness,
For they will be filled.
Blessed are the merciful,
For they will be shown mercy.
Blessed are the pure in heart,
For the will see God.
Blessed are the peace makers,
For they will be called sons of God.
Blessed are those who are persecuted because of righteousness,
For theirs is the kingdom of heaven.

Matthew 5: 3-10

THERE IS A TIME
FOR EVERYTHING.

There is a time for everything, a season for everything under heaven.

A time to be born and a time to die
A time to plant and a time to harvest
A time to kill and a time to heal
A time to tear down and a time to rebuild
A time to grieve and a time to dance
A time to scatter stones and a time to gather stone.
A time to embrace and a time to turn away
A time to search and a time to lose
A time to keep and a time to throw away
A time to tear and a time to mend
A time to be quiet and a time to speak up
A time to love and a time to hate
A time for war and a time for peace

Ecclesiastes 3:1:8

THE LORD IS MY SHEPHERD

The Lord is my shepherd. I shall not want.
He maketh me to lie down in green pastures; He leadeth me beside the still waters.

He restoreth my soul; He leadeth me in the paths of righteousness for His name's sake.

Yet though I walk through the valley of the shadow of death, I will fear no evil, for thou art with me, thy rod and thy staff, they comfort me,

Thou prepares a table before me in the presence of my enemies, thou annointest my head with oil, my cup runneth over,
Surely, goodness and mercy shall follow me all the days of my life and I will dwell in the house of the Lord forever

Psalm 23

Our Father

Our Father, who art in heaven,
hallowed be thy name.
Thy kingdom come,

thy will be done on earth as it is in heaven.
Give us this day our daily bread.
And forgive us our trespasses,

as we forgive those who trespass against us.
And lead us not into temptation,
but deliver us from evil.

Matthew 6: 9-13

SONGS YOU WILL
LOVE. I LOVE THEM.

Remember, that music soothes the soul. Feel the rhythm. Feel the beat and the harmony. Make a joyful noise and you will realize that music is a part of life. It is the key that opens the door.

Music expresses that which cannot be put into words and that which cannot remain silent.

Music is the speech of angels.

So my dear family and friends apply music in your prayers and you will have it all.

"Speak to one another with psalms, hymns and spiritual songs. Sing and make music in your heart to the Lord".

Ephesians 5:19

AMAZING GRACE

Amazing Grace, how sweet the sound,
That saved a wretch like me.
I once was lost but now am found,
Was blind, but now I see.

T'was Grace that taught my heart to fear.
And Grace, my fears relieved.
How precious did that Grace appear
The hour I first believed.

Though many dangers, toils and snares
I have already come;
'Tis Grace that brought me safe thus far
and Grace will lead me home.

The Lord has promised good to me.
His word my hope secures.
He will my shield and portion be,
As long as life endures.

When we've been there ten thousand years
Bright shining as the sun.
We've no less days to sing God's praise
Than when we've first begun

Yes, when this flesh and heart shall fail,
And mortal life shall cease;
I shall profess, within the vail, A life of joy and peace.

Isaiah 12:2

TAKE MY LIFE

Take my life and let it be
Concentrated Lord to thee
Take my moments and my days,
Let them flow in ceaseless praise.

I Surrender All

All to Jesus I surrender,
All to him I freely give;
I will ever love and trust him,
In his presence daily live.

MY GOD IS ABLE

My God is able, is able

I know He is able

I know my God is able to carry

me through.

IT IS WELL, IT IS WELL WITH MY SOUL

1. When peace, like a river, attendeth my way,
   When sorrows like sea billows roll;
   Whatever my lot, Thou has taught me to say,
   It is well, it is well, with my soul.

   Chorus:
   It is well, with my soul,
   It is well, it is well, with my soul.

2. Though Satan should buffet, though trials should come,
   Let this blest assurance control,
   That Christ has regarded my helpless estate,
   And hath shed His own blood for my soul.

3. My sin, oh, the bliss of this glorious thought!
   My sin, not in part but the whole,
   Is nailed to the cross, and I bear it no more,
   Praise the Lord, praise the Lord, O my soul!

4. And Lord, haste the day when the faith shall be sight,
   The clouds be rolled back as a scroll;
   The trump shall resound, and the Lord shall descend,
   Even so, it is well with my soul.

ON EAGLES WINGS

1. You who dwell in the shelter of the Lord
   Who abide in His shadow for life
   Say to the Lord
   "My refuge, my rock in whom I trust!"

   Chorus:
   And He will raise you up on eagles' wings
   Bear you on the breath of dawn
   Make you to shine like the sun
   And hold you in the palm of His hand.

2. The snare of the fowler will never capture you
   And famine will bring you no fear
   Under His wings your refuge
   His faithfulness your shield.

3. You need not fear the terror of the night
   Nor the arrow that flies by day
   Though thousands fall about you
   Near you it shall not come.

4. For to His angels He's given a command
   To guard you in all of your ways
   Upon their hands they will bear you up
   Lest you dash your foot against a stone.

   And He will raise you up on eagles' wings
   Bear you on the breath of dawn
   Make you to shine like the sun
   And hold you in the palm of His hand...

Be Not Afraid

You shall cross the barren desert, but you shall not die of thirst. You shall wander far in safety though you do not know the way.
You shall speak your words in foreign lands and all will understand.
You shall see the face of God and live.

Chorus

Be not afraid.
I go before you always.
Come follow me, and
I will give you rest.

If you pass through raging waters in the sea, you shall not drown.
If you walk amid the burning flames, you shall not be harmed.
If you stand before the power of hell and death is at your side, know that I am with you through it all.

Blessed are your poor, for the kingdom shall be theirs.
Blest are you that weep and mourn, for one day you shall laugh.
And if wicked men insult and hate you all because of me, blessed,
blessed are you!

Make Me A Channel
Of Your Peace

Make me a channel of your peace,
Where there is hatred let me bring your love,
Where there is injury, your pardon Lord,
And where there is doubt, true faith in you.

Make me a channel of your peace,

Where there's despair in life, let me bring hope,
Where there is darkness, only light,
And where there's sadness, ever joy.

Make me a channel of your peace,

It is in pardoning that we are pardoned,
In giving of ourselves that we receive.
And in dying that we are born to eternal life.

O Master grant that I may never seek,
So much to be consoled as to console,
To be understood as to understand,
To be loved as to love with all my soul.

WHATSOEVER YOU DO

Whatsoever you do to the least of my people,
That you do unto me

When I was hungry, you gave me to eat.
When I was thirsty, you gave me to drink.
Now enter into the home of My Father.

When I was homeless, you opened your door.
When I was naked, you gave me your coat.
Now enter into the home of My Father.

When I was weary, you helped me find rest.
When I was anxious, you calmed all my fears.
Now enter into the home of My Father.

When I was little, you taught me to read.
When I was lonely, you gave me your love.
Now enter into the home of My Father.

When In a prison, you came to my cell.
When on a sick bed, you cared for my needs.
Now enter into the home of My Father.

In a strange country, you made me at home,
Seeking employment, you found me a job.
Now enter into the home of My Father.

Hurt in a battle, you bound up my wounds.
Searching for kindness, you held out your hand.
Now enter into the home of My Father.

When I was Black, Latino or White,
Mocked and insulted, you carried my cross.
Now enter into the home of My Father.

When I was aged, you bothered to smile.
When I was restless, you listened and cared.
Now enter into the home of My Father.

You saw me covered with spittle and blood.
You knew my features, though grimy with sweat.
Now enter into the home of My Father.

When I was laughed at, you stood by my side.
When I was happy, you shared in my joy.
Now enter into the home of My Father.

It's Not An Easy Road

It's not an easy road
We are trav'ling to heaven,
For many are the thorns on the way;
It's not an easy road,
But the Savior is with us,
His presence gives us joy every day.

Chorus
No, no, it's not an easy road,
No, no, it's not an easy road;
But Jesus walks beside me
And brightens the journey,
And lifts my heavy burden this day.

It's not an easy road
There are trials and troubles
And many are the dangers we meet;
But Jesus guards and keeps
So that nothing can harm us,
And smooths the rugged path for our feet.

Though I am often footsore
And weary from travel,
Though I am often bowed down with care,
Well a better day is coming
When home in the glory
We'll rest in perfect peace over there.

ABIDE WITH ME

Abide with me; fast falls the eventide;
That darkness deepens; Lord with me abide.
When other helpers fail and comforts flee,
Help of the helpless, O abide with me.

Swift to its close ebbs out life's little day;
Earth's joys grow dim; its glories pass away;
Change and decay in all around I see;
O Thou who changest not, abide with me.

I need Thy presence every passing hour.
What but Thy grace can foil the tempter's power?
Who, like Thyself, my guide and stay can be?
Through cloud and sunshine, Lord, abide with me.

I fear no foe, with Thee at hand to bless;
Ill's have no weight, and tears no bitterness.
Where is death's sting? Where, grave, thy victory?
I triumph still, if Thou abide with me.

Hold Thou Thy cross before my closing eyes;
Shine through the gloom and point me to the skies.
Heaven's morning breaks, and earth's vain shadows flee;
In life, in death, O Lord, abide with me.

I FELT THAT THIS WILL BE A GOOD TIME TO DISCUSS OTHER THINGS THAT WILL ENERGIZE YOU, MAKE YOU FEEL HEALTHIER AND REGAIN HAPPINESS AGAIN AS THE DAYS GO BY. MOST OF THE TIME IN OUR LIVES WE DON'T READ, PRAY OR DO OTHER THINGS THAT MATTERS IN OUR LIFE UNTIL SOMETHING SERIOUS HAPPENS TO US. PLEASE, JOIN ME IN THIS SESSION TO EXPERIENCE OTHER THINGS THAT WILL HELP YOU TO PICK UP COURAGE, REGAIN HEALTH AND HAPPINNESSS AND CONTINUE ON WITH LIFE.

> "For whatever is born of God overcomes the world. And this is the victory that has overcome the world – our faith. Who is he who over comes the world, but he who believes that Jesus is the son of God."
>
> 1 John 5:4, 5

When you have faith, believed in your prayers by following the different types of praying steps, victory will set in and you will start picking up courage. This is the right time to start applying other things to help you regain energy, health and happiness back in your life.

DIFFERENT WAYS
TO PRAY:

Whatever you are praying for, know that the Lord is always there to listen and help you out.

"If you abide in Me, and my words abide in you, you will ask what you desire, and it shall be done for you."

And whatever things you ask in prayer, believing, you will receive. Whether you are praying for a good job, money, good relationship, a group to network with, success, health, status, wealth, beauty, children, recognition, appreciation, promotion or just peace of mind, pray and surrender it all to God, let him take charge and you will see it happening to you and happiness will start flowing in to overcome your sadness.

> "For the mountains shall depart and the hills removed, but my kindness shall not depart from you. Nor shall my covenant of peace be removed"
>
> Isaiah 54:10

FAITH'S STORY

A friend of mine Faith had a very bad experience when she lost her Dad. During the period she was very depressed, could not do anything or mingle with friends. We talked and I recommended a prayer book for her to read. She read it and she was so happy she did. She realized that she cannot change what has happened or bring back the dead Dad. She focused on her prayers looking for ways to make her self better. She focused on the prayers and gradually started recovering her energy, health and happiness back.

Once you build up that trust and surrender everything to God and start focusing on what you will do to generate happiness for yourself and others around you things starts getting better.

> "Abide in me and I in you. As the branch cannot bear fruit of itself, unless it abides in the vine, neither can you, unless you abide in me. I am the vine, you are the branches. He who abides in me, and I in him, bears much fruits, for without me, you cannot do nothing. If you abide in me, and my words abides in you, you will ask what you desire, and it shall be done for you"
>
> John 15: 4, 5, 7

The key here is that Faith was able to analyze the situation she was in and determined the best procedure to solve the problem. She did let go the fact that the dead Dad is not coming back and is also a thing of the past and focused on getting herself and everyone around her present back in shape by reading the prayer book, building her spirit, energizing herself and regaining happiness back to continue on life.

> "For the Lord God is a sun and shield; the Lord will give grace and glory; No good thing will He withhold from those who walk uprightly"
>
> Psalm 84:11

> "Meditate on these things; give yourself entirely to them, that your progress may be evident to all."
>
> 1 Timothy 4:15

GLAD'S STORY

Glad had the same situation but does not like to read, so I recommended meditation to her and informed her that with trust and faith she will be able to go through the situation and finally regain her courage and happiness. She started the meditation process I recommended, made it an important part of her day, and stayed connected to the Lord. She felt more at peace with her self, became healthier and happier.

Remember that when you make time to meditate which is any process that quiets your mind and helps you communicate in a sense of truth and love with your Lord. The process is very relaxing and enjoyable in that it creates a powerful effect on your body, mind and emotions. Meditating regularly will increase your level of happiness and reduce your stress level.

Here are some other ways to get connected:
Taking a walk
Being in nature
Listening to the sounds of the wind, birds and the flow of water
Sitting in silence
Listening to inspiring music.

> "Let your light so shine before men, that they may see your good works and glorify your faith in heaven"
>
> Matthew 5:14-16

LEARN TO MAKE PEACE WITH YOURSELF FIRST.

When you learn to make peace with yourself first, it benefits you and others around you.

Make peace with yourself by avoiding things that creates stress, anger and makes you unhappy, Example, complaining, blaming, and feeling ashamed or low self esteem. Instead, focus and accept positive things that build self esteem, identifying the gifts that others have that all of you can share and generate happiness. Start by changing the things you can change and those you cannot change, change your attitude towards them. Let go of the past, work with the present and if there is a present problem, define it, identify gifts and factors to solve the problem. Continue to make peace with yourself and others and you will experience increase in the level of happiness in you and those around you.

> "When you roam, they will lead you;
> When you sleep, they will keep you;
> And when you awake, they will speak with you.
> For the commandment are a lamp, and the law a light;
> Reproofs of instruction are the way of life
>
> Proverbs 6:22, 23

LET US REALIZE THAT WHAT WE WANT OR OUR THOUGHTS ARE NOT ALWAYS TRUE OR THE BEST FOR US.

BLESSING'S STORY

A friend of mine Blessing shared this story with me.

When she was young, she always had the feeling that she will one day be an Attorney. She likes to discuss and get peoples opinion about different things. Everything she was doing was focused on what she wants to be in life. She finished high school, went to University, but down the road, things started changing to another direction. Instead of the Attorney way which is a very nice profession that most of her friends also love, she started moving to the direction of a medical Doctor. She graduated from college, went to medical school and is now a Medical Doctor. I asked her, how it all happened, the change in the profession and a new her. She answered, "For years, I wanted something that was not for me and something happened in my life that made me to understand that our thoughts and wants are not always true or the best for us and that we don't have to believe everything we think but instead we should learn to examine our thoughts in a way that is best for our lives" The decision to become a Medical Doctor was very peaceful and also was the best for her with all glory and thanks to God.

> "Since you have purified your souls in obeying the truth through the spirit in sincere love of the brethren, love one another with a pure heart"
>
> 1 Peter 1:22

THE RELATIONSHIP BETWEEN TRUTH AND HAPPINESS

JOY'S STORY

I was discussing with Joy one day about her life and why she is always happy as nothing is ever wrong in her life. She said to me, my sister, the truth is that life does not have duplicate. I have come to live this life and the one that brought me into this world knows the best for me. Why will I worry myself over nothing? I have shifted and surrendered everything to Him and for Him to take charge of my life. She also mentioned that she has learnt to live by the truth and this sense of life generates peace in her and results in high level of energy, health and happiness.

Remember, that when you are truthful to each other, there is no space for fear and anxiety, the entire environment is filled with peace, love, hapiness and harmony.

> "Be kindly affectionate to one another with brotherly love, in honor giving preferences to one another; not lagging in diligence, fervent in spirit, serving the lord; distributing to the needs of the saints, given to hospitality"
>
> Romans 12:10, 11, 13

RELATIONSHIP BETWEEN BEHAVIOR, EXPRESSION AND HAPPINESS.

The power of a great smile.
Exchange great smile and warm greetings when you see each other. The smile in your face comes from your mind, your heart, your body, your soul, and the purpose is to make everyone around you feel at home and happy. When you exchange smiles and warm greetings to each other, the environment is peaceful, good spirit starts flowing, humor and friendliness prevails and everybody is happy.

SMILEY'S STORY

A friend of mine Smiley once told me that she attends a group event every once in a while and she has noticed that nobody likes to talk to her. I asked her, what do you do when you meet with the group? She said, I come in take my food, get a drink, sit and just enjoy myself and then live after the event. And I said, what do you do after you live the event? She said nothing. I then told her to smile at faces she makes eye contact with in her next meeting, give them a warm greeting and if possible move close to them, pick up a topic to discuss with them and make sure to get something from them that will make her remember who she had the conversation with. If it is a business meeting, get their business card, a religious, educational, or friendly group get their name, telephone number and e-mail to keep in touch after the group meeting.

She took my message and applied it to the next meetings and things started working for her. She called me and said, "Thank you. I did not know what a miracle just a smile can work in our lives. My present smiling face has worked a tremendous miracle in my life" I was very happy to hear from her and how a little step changed a situation.

> Bearing with one another, and forgiving one another, if anyone has a complaint against another, even as Christ forgave us, so you also must do"
> Colossians 3:13

THE RELATIONSHIP BETWEEN FORGIVENESS, LOVE AND HAPPINESS.

Seeking your happiness the right way is the best. I once asked a friend what makes her happy? She said to me, alcohol, gambling and watching a lot of television channel. I paused for a moment, and I asked again. Do these things really make you happy? She said, yes but after sometime the happiness disappears. Then I said to her, these sense of happiness is not right, and I suggested that she try positive sources that will help to increase her happiness level. Example, develop good relationship with family and friends, working on things that will make you to be successful, your financial security, enhancing your talent and strengths and above all connecting with your God on a regular basis. When you work with these factors, the positive results will energize you and in turn make you healthier and build your happiness level.

LOVE AND HAPPINESS

When you let love lead your life, love flows back. Let the juice in your heart flow so that you will experience greatness and happiness. Do not let fear factor in your life overcome your love factors like forgiveness, compassion and appreciation which will generate happiness while fear factors like anger, sadness, hurt and guilt will reduce your happiness level. Learn to focus on gratitude and practice forgiveness. Learn to wish others well. It will in turn create love and happiness. Realize that a heart overflowing with love is continually being filled with more love. Even in circumstances where people make you mad, wish them well and pay them back with kindness. Sharing love with one another, either silently, in words or actions, can have a tremendous effect on you and others. Do not underestimate the power we have to make someone else's day a little bit better by wishing them well and showing some light of love and kindness.

FORGIVENESS AND HAPPINESS

Forgiveness has been classed as one of the greatest form of love. Love is hard to lean to or practice when we are hurting because of something somebody did to us. But when we forgive and clean up, love flows in and happiness is always the end result. Forgive those that hate you or hurt you, treat them nice. Remember that when you forgive, you are given yourself a gift that allows your heart to be open, clean and welcome happiness. When you understand the suffering of others, it transforms your negative feelings with compassion and sets the stage for forgiveness to occur. Also when you forgive others, you are happier and stronger. You have better loving relationship, fewer health problems and less symptoms of stress.

THE POWER OF THANK YOU

Thank you. Two important words that out weights everything. Give thanks for everything that happens in your life for there is a reason for that. When you give thanks, more blessings will follow and in turn generate happiness for you. When you appreciate what others have done for you and give thanks to them, more rewards will flow your way.

RELATIONSHIP BETWEEN HEALTH AND HAPPINESS.

Eating the right food always play an important role in your happiness level. Eat nutritious food like whole foods, fruits and vegetables, fresh meat, fish, poultry, grains, Organic produce, dairy, natural sugar found in fruits, brown rice, whole grains, and regular green tea. This type of food will nourish and energize your body.

Avoid can foods, box food, packaged foods, white sugar, carbohydrate food, whole rice, pastries, flour, too much coffee and too much pop. Drink plenty of water.

Make sure to take enough rest. Having enough rest will energize your body.

Make sure to get at least 8 hours of sleep a day.

Make sure to exercise at least 15 minutes everyday. The exercise can be inform of walking, swimming, dancing etc. When you exercise, your brain receives more oxygen and courses your body to produce valuable chemicals and hormones that impact energy, mood, health and your happiness level.

Remember that when we are healthy, we are happier, when we are sick our happiness level is reduced. The way we eat, move, breath and our facial expression determines whether we are happy or not. When our body cells don't receive the support they need, the result is low energy and unhappiness. But when the cells receive what they need the result is high energy and happiness.

Avoid stress in your life. They can steal your happiness and health. Also learn to do things that make your cells strong and happy. Example, eating the right things, exercising, singing, listening to relaxing music, getting a massage, gardening, smiling and gardening raises our happiness level. Always remember that being happy is good for your health. Happiness and health go hand in hand. Improving one will in turn improve the other.

"Beloved, I pray that you prosper in all things and be in health, just as your soul prospers."

111 John 2

"For I will restore health to you and heal you of your wounds", says the Lord"

> "And so find favor and high esteem in the sight of God and man."
>
> Proverbs 3: 4

> "For the Lord God is a sun and shield; The Lord will give grace and glory; No good thing will he withhold from those who walk uprightly."
>
> Psalm 84:11

THE POWER OF PRAYER:

Finally, I must emphasis again the importance of prayers in our lives. In communicating with God, we are connected with energy bigger than ourself and the more deeply you experience the connection, the richer and more joyful your life feels. Realize that when you do everything in life with grace, you are connecting to God and creating health and happiness for yourself. Do not let other activities in your life prevent you from connecting, listening and speaking with your God. Even if it is only 5 minutes of silence, listening and talking to your God.

Develop a sense of surrendering all to your God. Trust in him to support you. Do not let your busy life make you to forget that if you surrender and put your faith, trust and hope in God, He will take charge and support you, and you will experience peace and happiness.

Let go of the past. Look into new ways to brighten your life and let happiness flow into your life. Read spiritual books that will inspire and add salt to your life.

Say no to the past and say yes to the present applying your faith, love and hope by choosing life that is meaningful and that can add to your health and happiness. When you hold on to your faith and trust in God, and continue to say yes to the present without even knowing what the result will be, surrendering and representing the present that you are in and putting everything in God's hand, He will take charge.

Remember that when you surrender it brings good to you. Why? Because you are no longer in charge and the Lord who is in charge will send you all that are good for you. I want you to look at this present, surrender and yes picture very well and how it can bring changes in your life that will result in increase in your level of happiness.

Always say in your prayers, I surrender all to you Lord. I seek your amazing grace that is infinite, your unconditional overflowing and gifted love. Ask Him for His will to be done and He will take charge.

> "Why worry, find happiness in life, for life does not have any duplicate"
>
> Florence Onochie

> "Truth has no fear and anxiety, instead it generates peace, love, happiness and harmony"
>
> Florence Onochie

"One love will keep all people of the world and God together"

Florence Onochie

"Surrender all and God will take charge of everything"

Florence Onochie

FLORENCE
ONOCHIE'S BIO

Florence Onochie is the president of FNO Professional Services Inc., and Vice President of HCO Inc., responsible for the management and the direction of the firms accounting, tax operations and computer-aided drafting and design department. She has worked in various managerial, teaching and accounting positions, including financial director to the director general IBC.

Florence have served as member and board member in several professional and humanitarian organizations, including the Rotary club, the Professional Women's advisory board, the National Association of Public Accountants, the National Association of Black Accountants, and National Association of Women Business Owners. She is also an Ambassador of the United States during World Forum, co founder of the International Women's review board, founder Florence Onochie Foundation International and IBC Hall of Fame.

In addition, Florence received numerous awards, Gold medal award for United States, Board of Governors Award, woman of the year in 2000, 2004, 2007 and International woman of the year 2010, Ambassador to the World Congress of Arts, Sciences and Communications, 2010 and was featured in Marquis Who's Who among American Women, Who's Who among Americans and Who's Who in the World. She has been featured in the Indianapolis Star, and the Indianapolis Recorder. She possesses degrees in accounting, finance and teachers training.

Florence is married with children.

ABOUT THE AUTHOR

Florence Onochie is one of those women that believes in inspiring and motivating others through inspirational and uplifting messages.

Florence is a renowned keynote speaker during National and International conferences and a great source for personal and professional development.

For her outstanding performance worldwide, she received numerous honors and awards.

Florence has written a lot of articles including books, magazines and calendars.

Her vast knowledge acquired from different field of studies and field of work continues to excel her on top when it comes to having diversified knowledge and experience towards education and life experience.

Florence's hope for you is that by the time you finish reading this book, your mind, soul and spirit will be renewed, and be filled with inspirational messages which in turn will encourage you to be strong and not be afraid, but to trust in God and continue on with life.

IMPORTANT CONTACTS

NAME _____   FAX _____

ADDRESS _____   CELLULAR _____

TELEPHONE _____   E-MAIL _____

NAME _____   FAX _____

ADDRESS _____   CELLULAR _____

TELEPHONE _____   E-MAIL _____

NAME _____   FAX _____

ADDRESS _____   CELLULAR _____

TELEPHONE _____   E-MAIL _____

NAME _____   FAX _____

ADDRESS _____   CELLULAR _____

TELEPHONE _____   E-MAIL _____

NAME _____   FAX _____

ADDRESS _____   CELLULAR _____

TELEPHONE _____   E-MAIL _____

NAME _____   FAX _____

ADDRESS _____   CELLULAR _____

TELEPHONE _____   E-MAIL _____

A Gift For You

FROM

_____

_____

TO

_____

_____

_____

REMAIN BLESSED

Important Notes

Important Contacts

NAME _____ FAX _____

ADDRESS _____ CELLULAR _____

TELEPHONE _____ E-MAIL _____

NAME _____ FAX _____

ADDRESS _____ CELLULAR _____

TELEPHONE _____ E-MAIL _____

NAME _____ FAX _____

ADDRESS _____ CELLULAR _____

TELEPHONE _____ E-MAIL _____

NAME _____ FAX _____

ADDRESS _____ CELLULAR _____

TELEPHONE _____ E-MAIL _____

NAME _____ FAX _____

ADDRESS _____ CELLULAR _____

TELEPHONE _____ E-MAIL _____

NAME _____ FAX _____

ADDRESS _____ CELLULAR _____

TELEPHONE _____ E-MAIL _____

IMPORTANT NOTES